The MUM who found her Sparkle

We would like to acknowledge the Traditional Custodians and Owners of the land we currently raise a family, work and play.

We would like to pay our respects to Elders past and present. We would also like to acknowledge any Aboriginal and Torres Strait Islander people who are reading this book today or working with us now or into the future.

This is, was and always will be Aboriginal land.

Acknowledgements

In November 2022, we ran a Kickstarter Campaign to fund the creation of this book. We couldn't have gotten to where we are without the people who supported us. This page is an acknowledgment of some of those people who helped us get to where we are today.

Elliott Family

Sparkle Dad Mitch, the brave Finley and the determined Ester

Sue Radnidge

Jessie's firecracker Mum, Nurse, Succulent Mum, Adventurer, Friend and Carer (And one proud Mama)

Peter and Tas Harpas

Mary's Kickass Parents

Kristy Purdon, Jessie's fabulous cousin

Team Purdon with Brad, Truth and Soul. Women In Mining QLD Inclusion and Diversity Champion

Lowndes Family

Stephen, Adriana and baby Zoi

Sotiropoulos Family

Sparkle Dad Bill and small but mighty Anastasia

Louise Miller

Account Executive, Fun Mum, Adventure Seeker (and our dancing Mama in the cream hoodie at the Glow Stick Party)

Keen Family

Rhianna, Wes, Dolcie, Fletcher & Elroy

Alex and Angela Manolaros

Marie Fisher

Mama, Teacher and Children's Entertainer Instagram- @mama_fairy_ (and our Mama at the Art Gallery)

This page serves as a ready-made web or network that Mamas can draw support from in their own Matrescence journey. If you're in need of some inspiration or support, any one of these women would be able to help in unlocking your own unique Sparkle. Matrescence never has to be done alone.

Regan Figg
Motherhood Coach, Pleasurepreneur
and Author of 'A Mother's Pleasure'
Instagram - @regan_figg

Julie Tenner
Intimacy and Relationship Coach
and Author of 'Flowers and Honey'
www.julietenner.love

Angela Christie
AC Clinical Hypnotherapy
'Making Waves to Change'
www.acclinicalhypnotherapy.com.au

Kirryn Lee
Matrescence Mentor, Energy Coach and host of the
Matrescence Awakening with Kirryn Lee podcast
www.kirrynlee.com

Coco Dee
CEO, Angel Investor and Founder
of the Female Financial Literacy Library
www.iamcocodee.com

Dr Sophie Brock
Motherhood Studies Sociologist and host
of The Good Enough Mother Podcast
www.drsophiebrock.com

Amy Taylor-Kabbaz
Matrescence Activist, Author
of 'Mama Rising' and Founder
of the Mama Rising Movement.
www.amytaylorkabbaz.com

'Mum, are you ok?' asked Oscar.

'No, I don't think so,' said Mum. 'I think my Sparkle may have disappeared.'

'Do you need help finding her?' asked Te *gently*.

'I think I might,' sighed Mum. 'I don't feel like me without her.'

'Well then, Mum, let's go! Let's go on an adventure to find your Sparkle!' yelled Oscar excitedly.

'Stop, stop! This looks like fun,' said Te, pointing.

'We might even find your Sparkle in here, Mum,' urged Oscar.

'That was so fun! I loved how the colours made rainbow faces everywhere,' beamed Te.

'Mum, what did you think?' asked Oscar.

'I liked, I liked…,' fumbled Mum. 'I liked how the music made me *feel* like the notes were dancing on my skin.'

'This way Mum. Something tells me we may be able to find your Sparkle in here,' insisted Oscar.

'My whole body is tingling. Check out these goosebumps!' exclaimed Mum.

'This one reminds me of you Mum,' said Oscar.

'Definitely,' agreed Te.

Mum smiled *cheekily*.

'You may be right.'

'Oscar, Te. Come and take a look. I've got an idea,' said Mum with a knowing smile.

'I know exactly where I'm going next,' said Mum *confidently*.

'Mum?' said Oscar, looking around.

'Where did she go?' asked Te.

Living as our sparkly selves can mean different things to different people. But really, it can be as simple as who we are in the world and what we enjoy doing.

When we get to do things we find fun, we feel better not just about ourselves, but others and the world. Our joy impacts everyone around us.

We know first-hand what it can be like to go through Matrescence and lose our sense of self; but please know, you are worthy of expressing yourself and finding your Sparkle.

Here are some questions for you to talk about with your family to help you find your own Sparkle, if it becomes lost. We would encourage you (if it feels good) to use this space to write or draw your sparkly days.

Conversations:

If you could spend your day however you wanted, what would you do?

_____
_____
_____

What is the most fun you have had as a family and why?

_____
_____
_____

What is your favourite piece of clothing to wear and why?

_____
_____
_____

What is something you have always wanted to do but haven't done?

_____
_____
_____

When in your day do you feel the most happy, inspired and sparkly?

_____

_____

_____

Big people reading this book, did you know we have an Instagram? We would love to hear about your experiences with this book and exploring the above questions. Please feel free to contact us or tag us over @themumwhofoundhersparkle.

We love hearing from our Sparkle fam!

Sparkly day memory

'MOTHERHOOD IS DIFFERENT TO MOTHERING

Mothering involves the tangible actions that are part of nurturing and raising a child, including acts such as feeding, bathing, caregiving, physical affection, and emotional support.

In contrast, Motherhood represents the broader social and cultural context within which mothers live and carry out their mothering. One crucial yet often overlooked influence that shapes the experiences of mothers is this broader cultural context and the unspoken rules about what it means to be a 'good mother'.

Many of these rules are not based on evidence around what is best for mothers, children, or families, but instead are based on a social stereotype about how mothers are supposed to think, act, behave, and feel.

Mothers are socialised to internalise many of these rules, and can feel overwhelming guilt when they feel they are unable to live up to these expectations.

Bringing awareness to the social context of Motherhood can help us push back against these social rules, and rewrite a version of Motherhood that centres our values, relationships, and authenticity.'

by Dr Sophie Brock, Motherhood Studies Sociologist

Helplines

Beyond Blue - 1300 22 4636

Gidget Foundation - 1300 851 758

Headspace - 1800 650 890

Kids Helpline - 1800 55 1800

Lifeline Australia - 13 11 14

Mensline Australia - 1300 78 99 78

PANDA - 1300 726 306

SANE - 1800 18 7263

Australian Breastfeeding Association - 1800 686 268

To all people, big or small, who are struggling to find

their Sparkle or creative expression,

we hope this book inspires you to look for it.

To our children, Finley, Ester and Anastasia,

our original Sparkle finders.

The ones who constantly remind us to look for magic in life

and inspire us to find joy in the simplest moments;

Thank you. This is all because of you.

To our fellow mamas navigating their own Matrescence journey, never discount your talents, interests or unique expression. Share your creativity with the world. We see you, we hear you, we are you.

Big love, Jessie and Mary

A special mention to Jessie's Dad, Peter Forbes, who may not have been here to support our journey, but who we know would have been incredibly proud to be a Sparkle Dad.

Sparkle HQ

First published by Sparkle HQ in 2023

This edition published in 2023

Cessnock & Goulburn, NSW, Australia

Text Copyright © Jessie Ann Elliott and Mary Sotiropoulos 2023

Illustrations Copyright © Jitumoni Goswami 2023

The moral right of the authors and illustrator has been asserted.

All rights reserved. No part of this publication may be reproduced without prior permission of the publisher.

A catalogue record for this book is available from the National Library of Australia

ISBN: 978-0-646-88683-1

www.the-mum-who-found-her-sparkle.ck.page/31c7b7dfc1

www.ingramcontent.com/pod-product-compliance
Lightning Source LLC
Chambersburg PA
CBHW041200290426
44109CB00002B/75